Couples Ultimate Handbook: Elevating Communication, Intimacy and Sex

MAVEN PRESS

Copyright © Laura Elizabeth
First published in Australia in 2024
by Maven Press
Roleystone WA 6111

Cover Design by Laura Elizabeth
Edited by Jade Bell

All rights reserved. No part of this book may be used or reproduced by any means, graphic, electronic, or mechanical, including photocopying, recording, taping or by any information storage retrieval system without the written permission of the copyright owner except in the case of brief quotations embodied in critical articles and reviews.

Because of the dynamic nature of the Internet, any web addresses or links contained in this book may have changed since publication and may no longer be valid. The views expressed in this work are solely those of the author and do not necessarily reflect the views of the publisher and the publisher hereby disclaims any responsibility for them.

A catalogue record for this work is available from the National Library of Australia

National Library of Australia Catalogue-in-Publication data:
Couples Ultimate Handbook: Elevating Communication, Intimacy and Sex/Laura Elizabeth

ISBN: 978-0-9756174-4-1
(Print)
ISBN: 978-0-9756174-5-8
(Ebook)

Couples Ultimate Handbook: Elevating Communication, Intimacy and Sex

Meet Laura Elizabeth, a visionary trailblazer and fervent advocate for intimacy and connection: bestselling author, publisher and director of Laura Elizabeth Wellness.In her mission to empower conscious couples, Laura is committed to crafting intimate experiences that invite a profound understanding of self. Her guidance enables couples to embrace and embody their sensuality, reclaim their voices, and authentically wield their power to fuel meaningful, lasting relationships. As a devoted single mother of three, Laura leads by example, consistently achieving and surpassing her goals while living purposefully and unwaveringly. She aspires to positively influence her children and inspire others to unlock their full potential and live deeply connected, pleasure-filled lives.

The *Couples Ultimate Handbook*, a comprehensive guide designed to enhance the connection between partners by fostering better communication, deeper intimacy and a more fulfilling sexual relationship. You will find a wealth of interactive ideas and activities in this handbook to help strengthen the bonds that make your relationship unique.

Chapter 1: Foundation of Communication

Communication is the bedrock of building strong and resilient relationships. It is the lifeline connecting partners, allowing them to share thoughts, feelings, and dreams. In this chapter, we'll delve into the essential components of effective communication and provide practical tools to strengthen the foundation of your relationship.

The Power of Active Listening

Listening is an art. Often, we listen not to understand but to respond. Active listening, however, involves fully concentrating, understanding, responding, and remembering what your partner is saying.

Practical Exercise: Reflective Listening

Choose a Conversation Topic

Select a topic you both feel comfortable discussing. It could be about your day, plans, or a shared interest.

Practice Reflective Listening

When your partner speaks, reflect on what you've heard before responding. For example, 'What I'm hearing is…' or 'It sounds like you're saying …'

Switch Roles:
Exchange roles and allow your partner to practice reflective listening. Discuss the experience and how it felt to be genuinely heard.

The Art of Effective Expression
Communication is a two-way street. Openly expressing your thoughts and feelings is as crucial as listening. Honesty, vulnerability and clarity pave the way for understanding.

Practical Exercise: The Feelings Jar

Create a Feelings Jar:
Set up a jar filled with emotive words written on slips of paper. Use this as a tool to help articulate your feelings.

Daily Emotion Check-Ins:
At the end of each day, randomly pick an emotion slip from the jar and share a moment from your day related to that emotion. Doing this encourages emotional expression and vulnerability.

Navigating Through Disagreements
Conflict is inevitable. However, the way we manage conflicts defines the health of a relationship. Constructive conflict resolution involves active listening, expressing needs, and finding common ground.

Practical Exercise: The 'I' Statements Technique

Express Using 'I' Statements:
Instead of saying 'you always' or 'you never,' express your feelings and needs using 'I' statements. For example, 'I feel upset when…' or 'I need…'

Practice Active Listening During Conflicts:
When conflicts arise, actively listen to your partner's perspective before responding. Avoid interrupting and seek to understand their point of view.

The Role of Non-Verbal Communication
Actions often speak louder than words. Non-verbal cues, such as body language and facial expressions, are significant in conveying emotions.

Practical Exercise: Non-Verbal Connection Rituals

Establish Non-Verbal Connection Moments:
Create rituals that involve non-verbal communication, such as holding hands during walks, maintaining eye contact during conversations, or a simple touch on the shoulder.

Reflect on Non-Verbal Cues
Take time to reflect on each other's non-verbal cues. Discuss what gestures make you feel most connected and understood.

Consistency and Rituals in Communication
Consistency builds trust. Establishing regular communication rituals fosters a sense of security and reinforces your emotional connection.

Practical Exercise: Daily Check-Ins

Scheduled Daily Check-Ins:
Set aside a specific time each day for a brief check-in. Discuss your highs and lows, share something you appreciate about each other, or express something you hope for the next day.

Reflect on the Impact
After a week of daily check-ins, reflect on the impact on your connection. Discuss how this practice has influenced your understanding of each other.

Communication is not a destination but a journey—a continual exploration of understanding and connection. As you navigate this journey together, remember that the foundation of communication is not only about words but also the intention, attention and commitment you bring to each interaction.

By honing these skills, you lay the groundwork for a relationship that thrives on openness, understanding, and love.

Understanding Each Other's Love Languages
In the intricate dance of love, communication is the music that guides the steps, and understanding each other's love languages is the key to an elegant performance. Dr Gary Chapman's concept of love languages provides a framework for unravelling the mystery of how individuals express and receive love. In this chapter, we'll explore the significance of love languages and guide you through practical exercises to discover and embrace your partner's unique language.

The Five Love Languages

Words of Affirmation:
Individuals who appreciate Words of Affirmation thrive on verbal expressions of love. Compliments, encouraging words, and affirmations make their hearts soar.

Quality Time:
For those with Quality Time as their love language, nothing says 'I love you' like undivided attention. Meaningful conversations and shared ex-

periences build the connection they crave.

Receiving Gifts:
The language of love for some is wrapped in thoughtful presents. It's not about the price tag but the sentiment and effort behind the gift.

Acts of Service:
Actions speak louder than words for individuals with Acts of Service as their love language. Performing tasks or helpful acts demonstrates love and commitment.

Physical Touch:
The language of Physical Touch speaks through hugs, kisses, and physical closeness. Touch is a powerful way to convey love and affection for these individuals.

Discovering Your Partner's Love Language
Pay attention to how your partner expresses love and what actions or words bring them the most joy.

Have an open and honest conversation about love languages. Share your observations and discuss which expressions of love resonate most with both of you.

Take the official *Love Language Quiz* together. This interactive tool provides insights into your primary and secondary love languages.

Practical Exercise: Love Language Letters

Write a Love Letter:
Take time to individually write a heartfelt love letter to your partner expressing your feelings and appreciation.

Highlight Love Language Elements:

In your letters, incorporate aspects of your partner's love language. For example, if their love language is Words of Affirmation, focus on expressing love through words.

Exchange the letters and take time to read them together. Discuss the elements that resonated most and why.

Applying Love Languages in Daily Life

Daily Affirmations:

Incorporate daily affirmations that align with your partner's love language. A simple 'I love you' or a compliment can go a long way.

Quality Time Rituals:

Establish routines for spending quality time together, whether it's a weekly date night, morning coffee chats, or an evening walk.

Acts of Service Surprises:

Surprise your partner with acts of service that cater to their needs or desires. It could be as simple as taking care of a household chore or preparing a special meal.

Thoughtful Gifts:

Occasional thoughtful gifts, even small ones, can speak volumes. Consider your partner's interests and preferences when selecting gifts.

Physical Touch Rituals:

Create rituals that involve physical touch, such as holding hands during a movie night or sharing a hug before parting ways in the morning.

Understanding and embracing each other's love languages is a powerful step toward creating a fulfilling and harmonious relationship. As you embark on this journey of discovery, remember that love languages can evolve, and maintaining open communication ensures that your expressions of love remain attuned to each other's changing needs.

Daily Check-Ins: Five-Minute Conversations

Absolutely! A five-minute daily check-in is a simple and practical way for a couple to connect, share, and stay attuned to each other's thoughts and feelings.

Here's an example template for a quick and meaningful daily check-in:

Daily Check-In for Couples: Five Minutes

Share a Highlight:

Each partner takes turns sharing the highlight or positive aspect of their day. It could be a small accomplishment, a pleasant surprise, or a moment of joy.

Partner 1: 'My highlight today was receiving a compliment from my colleague for a project I've been working on.'

Partner 2: 'That's fantastic! I'm so proud of you. My highlight was having a great conversation with a friend during lunch.'

Express a Challenge:

Next, discuss any challenges or difficulties encountered during the day. This is an opportunity to share and provide support.

Partner 1: 'I felt a bit overwhelmed with the workload today. I'm struggling to find a balance.'

Partner 2: 'I'm here for you. Let's talk more about how we can manage that together. My challenge was dealing with unexpected changes at work.'

Share Something You're Grateful For:
Take a moment to express gratitude. This can be related to each other, the day's experiences, or something in general.

Partner 1: 'I'm grateful for your support and understanding during stressful times. It means a lot to me.'

Partner 2: 'I'm grateful for our cozy dinner. It's those moments that make everything better.'

Discuss Tomorrow's Plans:
Briefly discuss the plans or goals for the next day. This can help both partners align their expectations and provide an opportunity for collaboration.

Partner 1: 'I have an early meeting tomorrow, so I'll need to focus on preparing tonight.'

Partner 2: 'I'll make sure to keep the evening calm and support you in any way you need.'

End with a Positive Affirmation:
Close the check-in on a positive note. Share a word of encouragement, love, or appreciation.

Partner 1: 'I appreciate you and the love we share. Goodnight.'

Partner 2: 'I love you too. Sleep well and sweet dreams.'

Remember, keeping it brief, focused, and supportive is the key. Adjust the questions and topics based on your preferences and what feels most relevant daily. This daily practice fosters connection, understanding, and emotional intimacy within the relationship.

Chapter 2: Interactive Communication Tools

Interactive communication tools for couples offer innovative and engaging ways to deepen understanding, strengthen connections, and foster a sense of shared experiences. These tools enhance communication and provide a playful and dynamic avenue for couples to navigate challenges, celebrate successes, and continually grow together. By incorporating interactive communication tools into their routine, couples can create a shared digital space that nurtures intimacy and strengthens the foundation of their relationship.

Journaling: Sharing Thoughts & Dreams

Couples journaling is a powerful and intimate practice that invites partners to share their thoughts, dreams, and emotions within the pages of a shared journal.

This shared endeavour goes beyond mere communication, fostering a deeper understanding and connection between partners.

The act of putting pen to paper encourages vulnerability, as each partner contributes to the evolving narrative of their relationship. Couples can use the journal to express gratitude, set goals, and reflect on shared experiences. It becomes a tangible record of their journey, serving as a testament to their growth as individuals and as a couple. This intentional practice of couples journaling strengthens communication. It provides a unique and lasting keepsake that captures the essence of their love story.

Journaling Exercise: Exploring Shared Dreams

Set aside a quiet evening for this couples journaling exercise. Begin by choosing a journal that you both find appealing, perhaps with blank pages or prompts that resonate with your journey. Find a cozy and comfortable space to sit together, away from distractions.

Reflect on Your Individual Dreams:

Start by individually reflecting on your personal dreams and aspirations. Take a few minutes to write down what you envision for your future, both as an individual and within the relationship. Consider career goals, personal growth, travel desires, and any other aspirations that come to mind.

Once you've had time to reflect, take turns sharing your dreams. Be open and honest, and use this time to deepen your understanding of each other's aspirations. Discuss any common themes or goals that emerge.

Identify Shared Dreams:

Explore the possibilities of dreams that you both share. These could be goals related to your relationship, such as building a family, travelling together, or creating a home. Note down these shared dreams in your couple's journal.

Create a Vision Board or Collage:

Get creative by turning your shared dreams into a visual representation. Use magazines, images, or drawings to create a vision board or collage within your journal. This visual reminder will be a powerful and inspiring representation of your shared aspirations.

Write a Letter to Your Future Selves:
In the journal, write a letter to your future selves, expressing your commitment to working towards these shared dreams. Include the steps you plan to take, the support you'll provide each other, and the excitement you feel envisioning these dreams becoming a reality.

Regularly Revisit and Update:
Make this couple's journaling exercise an ongoing practice. Set a regular time, perhaps once a month or quarterly, to revisit your shared dreams, update your progress, and adjust your aspirations as needed.

This couple's journaling exercise strengthens your connection and provides a roadmap for navigating your shared journey. It's a beautiful way to align your visions, foster support, and create a tangible representation of the dreams that bind you together.

Vision Board: Creating a Shared Future
A vision board is a visual representation of one's aspirations, goals, and desires, created by compiling images, words, and affirmations on a board or poster. It is a powerful tool for manifesting dreams and focusing on specific objectives.

Typically, a vision board includes images and phrases that resonate with the individual's or group's aspirations, from personal development and career goals to travel plans and lifestyle choices.

The process of creating a vision board involves thoughtful reflection, collaboration, and creativity as individuals or groups carefully curate a collection of visuals that inspire and motivate. A vision board is displayed prominently as a daily reminder of the desired future, fostering a positive mindset and serving as a tangible representation of the journey toward personal or collective aspirations.

Chapter 3: Deepening Intimacy

Deepening intimacy within a couple is a deliberate process that fosters emotional, physical, and relational closeness. It requires an open and vulnerable exchange of thoughts and feelings, creating a safe space where both partners can express their authentic selves without judgment. Effective communication is at the heart of this journey, encouraging active listening and understanding. Emotional intimacy often grows when couples share their dreams, fears, and vulnerabilities, establishing a profound connection. Physical intimacy, encompassing both affectionate touch and sexual expression, is another integral aspect. Intentional moments of closeness, through shared experiences, rituals, or simple gestures, contribute to the depth of a couple's bond. Building trust, practising gratitude, and maintaining a sense of curiosity about each other's inner worlds all contribute to the ongoing process of deepening intimacy, ultimately enriching the fabric of the relationship.

Exploring Emotional Intimacy: Vulnerability Exercises

Emotional Vulnerability Exchange:
Sit facing each other and take turns sharing a significant and vulnerable

emotion or experience from your past. The key is to express yourself openly and authentically, allowing your partner to witness your vulnerability. After each sharing, the listener responds with empathy and validation, creating a space of emotional intimacy. This exercise fosters deep connection and understanding between partners.

Guided Sensory Exploration:
Create a quiet and comfortable space where you and your partner can engage in guided sensory exploration. Blindfold one partner while the other uses various textures, scents, and sounds to evoke sensations. The blindfolded partner relies on trust and vulnerability, heightening their awareness of touch, smell, and sound. Afterwards, switch roles and discuss the experience. This exercise deepens physical intimacy and fosters a sense of vulnerability and trust.

Fear and Desire Mapping:
Sit together and individually create lists of your fears and desires both within and outside the relationship. These can range from personal fears and aspirations to those related to the relationship itself.

Share your lists, discussing the emotions and experiences behind each item. This exercise cultivates vulnerability by exposing deep-seated fears and desires, encouraging mutual understanding and support.

Note: While these exercises can enhance emotional intimacy, it's essential to approach them with sensitivity and respect for each other's comfort levels. Always communicate openly about boundaries and ensure that both partners feel safe during these vulnerable moments.

Non-Sexual Touch: A Week-Long Challenge
Non-sexual touch holds profound significance in fostering emotional intimacy and building a solid foundation within a relationship. It encompasses a spectrum of tactile expressions, from simple gestures like

holding hands and hugs to more nuanced touches such as gentle caresses or supportive pats.

The benefits of non-sexual touch are manifold. It releases oxytocin, the 'bonding hormone,' promoting feelings of trust and connection. This physical closeness also reduces stress and anxiety, creating a sense of comfort and security.

Beyond the physiological aspects, non-sexual touch is a powerful form of communication, conveying love, empathy, and understanding without the need for words. It enhances emotional well-being, nurtures a deeper connection between partners, and is crucial in maintaining a healthy and thriving relationship.

7-Day Non-Sexual Touch Challenge: Cultivating Intimacy Through Physical Connection

Day 1: Hand-Holding Harmony
Start the challenge with the simple yet powerful act of holding hands. Let your hands intertwine, whether taking a stroll, watching a movie, or simply sitting together. Pay attention to the warmth and connection this fundamental touch brings.

Day 2: Shoulder to Lean On
Offer each other a supportive touch by resting your head on your partner's shoulder or vice versa. This physical closeness creates a sense of security and comfort, reinforcing your emotional connection.

Day 3: Affectionate Back Rubs
Take turns giving each other gentle back rubs. This non-sexual touch promotes relaxation and intimacy. Use soothing motions and focus on creating a sense of care and tenderness.

Day 4: Heartfelt Hugging
Embrace each other in a prolonged hug. Let the hug convey a genuine sense of love and appreciation. Take a moment to breathe together, syncing your heartbeats and fostering a deep emotional connection.

Day 5: Intimate Forehead Kisses
Explore the tender act of giving and receiving forehead kisses. This gesture communicates affection and admiration, emphasizing the emotional bond you share.

Day 6: Hand Tracing Connection
Sit facing each other and take turns tracing the lines on each other's palms with your fingertips. This intricate touch fosters a unique connection and enhances mindfulness about the subtleties of physical contact.

Day 7: Mutual Foot Massages
Conclude the challenge with a relaxing foot massage session. Create a tranquil environment, use soothing lotions, and take turns pampering each other's feet. This activity promotes relaxation and reinforces the idea of nurturing through touch.

Throughout the challenge, emphasise communication and attentiveness to each other's comfort levels. The goal is to deepen emotional intimacy through non-sexual touch, creating a foundation of physical connection that strengthens your overall relationship.

Chapter 4: Building Trust

Building trust within a relationship is a delicate yet foundational process that requires time, consistency, and open communication. Trust evolves through transparent honesty, where partners feel safe being vulnerable without fear of judgment. It is nurtured by reliability, keeping promises, showing up for each other, and consistently demonstrating commitment.

Active listening and empathetic understanding play pivotal roles, allowing partners to feel heard and validated. Trust is also strengthened by setting and respecting boundaries and cultivating a sense of emotional safety. As couples navigate challenges together with mutual support and understanding, trust becomes the bedrock of their connection, creating a resilient foundation for a healthy and lasting relationship.

Trust-Building Games: Strengthening Emotional Bonds

The Trust Fall Challenge:

In a safe and open space, one partner stands with their back to the other. The partner facing away closes their eyes and falls backward, trusting their partner to catch them.

This physical activity fosters both trust and communication, as the catching partner learns to anticipate and respond to their partner's movements. After each round, discuss the feelings and emotions that arose during the exercise.

The Shared Story Game:
Set aside time for a storytelling session where each partner takes turns sharing personal experiences, thoughts, or dreams.

The challenge is to be vulnerable and open about aspects of their lives they may not have discussed. This game encourages trust-building through shared narratives, creating a deeper understanding of each other's histories and fostering connection.

The Blindfolded Guiding Challenge:
One partner wears a blindfold while the other guides them through a simple obstacle course or around the home. The blindfolded partner must rely entirely on their partner's verbal instructions and physical guidance. This game builds trust by emphasising effective communication and reliance on each other. After the challenge, switch roles to reinforce the importance of trust and communication in navigating life's obstacles together.

Transparency Talks:
Honest Conversations for a Solid Foundation Transparency talks in a relationship involve open and honest conversations where partners willingly share their thoughts, feelings and experiences. These discussions create a foundation of trust, allowing both individuals to be vulnerable without fear of judgment.

An example of a transparency talk might revolve around sharing personal goals and aspirations. For instance, one partner could express a desire for career advancement.

At the same time, the other discusses their goal of personal growth through a new hobby. They can align their aspirations, offer support, and collaboratively plan their future through transparent communication.

These talks deepen understanding and strengthen the emotional bond by fostering an environment where both partners feel heard, accepted, and valued.

Chapter 5: Spice Up Your Sex Life

A spicy and fulfilling sex life holds immense importance within a romantic relationship, serving as a dynamic and integral component of overall intimacy. Beyond the physical pleasure it provides, a healthy sexual connection contributes significantly to emotional bonding, trust, and overall relationship satisfaction.

Intimacy in the bedroom fosters a sense of vulnerability and openness, creating a unique space for partners to communicate and explore each other's desires.

A spicy sex life is not only an expression of passion but also a source of stress relief, promoting physical and emotional well-being. Investing in this aspect of a relationship keeps the flame alive, reigniting the initial spark and ensuring that partners continue to prioritise and enjoy each other's company on a profound and pleasurable level.

Regular and adventurous intimacy is a testament to the vitality of a relationship, enhancing the connection and contributing to the overall happiness and longevity of the partnership.

Communication in the Bedroom: Discussing Desires and Boundaries

Fantasy Jar Exploration:
Create a 'Fantasy Jar' together, where each partner writes down their sexual fantasies on separate pieces of paper. These can range from mild to adventurous. Take turns picking a fantasy from the jar and discussing your thoughts and feelings.

This exercise provides a structured and playful way to explore desires without judgment, encouraging open communication about fantasies and preferences.

Desire Mapping Exercise:
Sit together and create a 'Desire Map'.

Draw a spectrum, with one end representing activities or aspects you both enjoy and the other end representing things you are curious or intrigued about. Discuss and place various intimate desires on this spectrum. This visual representation allows for a conversation about desires, providing insight into shared interests and areas where exploration might be welcomed.

The Yes, No, Maybe List:
Compile a list of various intimate activities, fantasies, or scenarios. Each partner goes through the list and categorises items as 'Yes' (definitely interested), 'No' (not interested), or 'Maybe' (open to discussion). Share your lists and discuss the reasons behind your choices. This exercise reveals shared interests, helps establish clear boundaries, and promotes open dialogue about desires.

In all these exercises, the key is to approach the conversation with sensitivity, respect, and a non-judgmental attitude. Creating a safe space for discussing desires allows partners to openly communicate their preferences, fostering a deeper understanding and connection in the bedroom.

Sensate Focus Exercises: Heightening Sensual

Awareness

Sensate focus exercises are a series of structured activities designed to enhance sensory awareness and communication between partners, particularly in the realm of physical intimacy. These exercises are often used in couples therapy to reconnect and build intimacy. The focus is on deliberately and attentively exploring touch, sensation, and emotional responses.

Example 1: Progressive Body Scan

Partners take turns exploring each other's bodies with their hands. The emphasis is on touch without a specific goal or outcome. Start with non-sexual touch and gradually progress to more intimate areas. The goal is to foster awareness, communication, and responsiveness to each other's cues.

Example 2: Mutual Massage

Engage in a shared massage experience where both partners give and receive massages. Use different textures, pressures, and techniques to explore sensations. The emphasis is on relaxation, connection and communication through touch rather than a focus on sexual performance.

Example 3: Guided Sensory Exploration

One partner is blindfolded while the other guides them through a sensory experience. This could involve using various textures and scents or even tasting different foods.

The blindfolded partner focuses on heightened sensory awareness and the emotional responses elicited by each sensation. Afterward, roles are reversed.

These exercises promote mindfulness, communication, and the development of a deeper understanding of each other's bodies and desires. The aim is to create a non-judgmental and open space for partners to connect on a sensory level, fostering a more intimate and satisfying physical relationship.

Chapter 6: Exploring Fantasies Together

Sexual fantasies are a natural and intricate aspect of human sexuality, encompassing a wide range of desires, scenarios, and imaginings that individuals may find arousing or intriguing. These fantasies can be diverse, from the mildly adventurous to the more elaborate and fantastical. They often serve as a means of self-exploration, allowing individuals to understand their desires, preferences, and boundaries in intimacy.

Importantly, sexual fantasies are a personal and private aspect of one's inner world, contributing to the richness and complexity of human sexuality. While some fantasies may be shared between partners to enhance communication and intimacy, it's crucial to approach such discussions with respect, understanding, and a non-judgmental attitude, recognizing that fantasies are a normal and healthy part of sexual expression.

Fantasy Jar: A Safe Space for Shared Desires (see above)

Role-Play Adventures: Stepping into Each

Other's Fantasies

Role-playing is a form of sexual or intimate exploration where individuals or partners take on specific roles or personas to enhance arousal, creativity, and intimacy. It allows for a playful and imaginative approach to intimacy, often breaking away from routine and adding an element of novelty to the sexual experience.

Example 1: Power Dynamic Role Play

Partners may choose roles that involve a power dynamic, such as a boss and employee or a teacher and student. The power imbalance adds an element of excitement and novelty, allowing both individuals to explore different facets of their sexuality within a consensual and agreed-upon context.

Example 2: Fantasy Scenario Role Play

Couples can engage in role-playing scenarios based on shared fantasies or interests. This could involve creating characters or situations that fulfil specific desires, such as a chance encounter in a bar, a romantic rendezvous, or even a scenario where partners meet as strangers and embark on a thrilling adventure.

In role-playing, communication is key to ensure both partners are comfortable with the chosen roles and scenarios. Establishing clear boundaries, using safe words, and checking in with each other afterward contribute to a positive and consensual role-playing experience. It's a creative and enjoyable way to explore different aspects of intimacy and enhance the connection between partners.

Chapter 7: Mutual Growth and Development

Mutual growth and development within a relationship are vital components that contribute to the resilience and satisfaction of a partnership. This process involves both individuals evolving and flourishing together, not just as a result of shared experiences but also through individual pursuits. It entails supporting each other's personal goals, aspirations, and self-discovery journeys. As partners invest in their own growth, they bring newfound insights, strengths, and resilience to the relationship. This mutual commitment to individual and collective development fosters a dynamic and evolving connection. Communication is crucial, allowing partners to express their evolving needs, dreams, and challenges. By navigating the twists and turns of personal and shared growth, couples fortify their bond and create a foundation for a relationship that flourishes amidst the ongoing journey of self-discovery and mutual development.

Setting Goals: Aligning Your Aspirations

How to Set Couples Goals Together: A Step-by-Step Guide

Setting couples goals is a meaningful way to foster connection, alignment, and shared aspirations within a relationship.

Follow these steps to collaboratively define and pursue your goals as a couple:

Schedule a Goal-Setting Session
Dedicate uninterrupted time for a goal-setting discussion. Choose a quiet, comfortable space where you can both focus on the conversation without distractions.

Reflect on Individual Goals
Begin by individually reflecting on your personal goals. Consider short-term and long-term aspirations, covering various aspects such as career, personal development, relationships, and lifestyle.

Share and Discuss
Take turns sharing your individual goals. Discuss the motivations behind your goals, any challenges you foresee, and how these aspirations align with your values and priorities.

Identify Shared Goals
Explore the overlap between your individual goals and identify those that you both share or can align with. These shared goals form the foundation for your couple's goals.

Prioritise and Set SMART Goals
Prioritise the identified shared goals and convert them into Specific, Measurable, Achievable, Relevant, and Time-Bound (SMART) objectives. This ensures clarity and practicality in your goal-setting.

Break Down Larger Goals
If your shared goals are substantial, break them down into smaller, manageable steps. This makes the goals more achievable and provides a roadmap for progress.

Create a Vision Board or List
Visualize your couples' goals by creating a vision board or a list. Use images, words, or symbols that represent your shared aspirations. Display this visual representation where you can both revisit it regularly.

Establish a Timeline
Set a realistic timeline for achieving your couple's goals. Define milestones and deadlines for each step, helping you stay on track and celebrate progress together.

Discuss Roles and Responsibilities
Clearly define the roles and responsibilities of each partner in working towards the shared goals. This ensures that both individuals actively contribute to the pursuit of these aspirations.

Regularly Review and Adjust
Schedule periodic reviews to discuss the progress of your couple's goals. Be open to adjusting or refining them based on changing circumstances, evolving priorities, or new opportunities.

By approaching couples goal-setting with open communication, mutual understanding, and a shared vision, you lay the groundwork for a relationship that thrives on shared aspirations and continuous growth.

Chapter 8: Adventure and Playfulness

Adventure and playfulness inject a vibrant energy into a relationship, creating an atmosphere of joy, spontaneity, and shared excitement. Embracing adventure together involves stepping outside comfort zones, whether it's trying new activities, exploring unfamiliar places, or embarking on spontaneous journeys.

Conversely, playfulness encompasses lightheartedness, laughter and a willingness to engage in whimsical or silly moments. These elements infuse a relationship with a sense of novelty and serve as a catalyst for a deeper connection.

Whether engaging in playful banter, taking on new challenges together, or embarking on thrilling adventures, couples find that the shared experiences of joy and discovery enhance their bond and create lasting memories. Adventure and playfulness become the threads that weave a tapestry of shared happiness and resilience within a relationship.

Surprise Date Nights: Keep Romance Alive

Surprise date nights are a delightful way to add spontaneity and excitement to a relationship. They involve one partner planning and executing a surprise outing or activity for the other, creating an element of mystery and anticipation. These surprise experiences can range from simple and intimate to elaborate and adventurous, tailored to the couple's preferences. The element of surprise heightens the sense of connection and keeps the romance alive.

Here are five examples of surprise date nights:

Picnic Under the Stars
Prepare a basket with your partner's favorite snacks, a cozy blanket, and a stargazing guide. Take your partner to a scenic spot, whether it's a local park or a secluded beach and enjoy a romantic picnic under the stars.

Mystery Dinner Date
Blindfold your partner and lead them to a carefully chosen restaurant or a beautifully set-up dinner at home. Keep the menu a secret until they arrive, adding an element of surprise to the dining experience.

Scavenger Hunt Adventure
Create a personalised scavenger hunt that takes your partner to meaningful places or recalls special memories. Each clue can lead them to the next location, culminating in a surprise activity or destination.

Themed Movie Night at Home
Transform your living room into a cozy cinema with a surprise movie marathon featuring your partner's favourite films or a theme that holds sentimental value. Prepare some popcorn and snacks, and create a comfy movie-watching atmosphere.

Hot Air Balloon Ride at Sunrise
Arrange a surprise hot air balloon ride at dawn for an unforgettable and breathtaking experience. Watch the sunrise together from the sky, creat-

ing a memory that will linger as a symbol of your shared sense of adventure.

Surprise date nights are all about creating memorable moments and expressing thoughtfulness in unexpected ways. The key is to tailor the surprise to your partner's interests and preferences, ensuring that each surprise date night is a unique and cherished experience.

Bucket List: Exploring New Horizons

A couples' bucket list is a compilation of shared dreams, experiences and goals a pair endeavours to accomplish together. Crafting one involves joint exploration, imaginative brainstorming, and a shared commitment to creating memorable moments.

Here's a step-by-step guide on how to create a couples' bucket list:

Shared Reflection

Begin by individually jotting down your personal aspirations, whether they relate to travel, personal growth, or shared adventures. Reflect on your dreams and identify what resonates with both of you.

Open Dialogue

Share your individual reflections with your partner. Engage in open and honest conversations about the aspirations that excite both of you. Discuss the significance of each goal and how it aligns with your vision for the relationship.

Identify Common Themes

Look for common themes and interests that emerge from your discussions. These shared elements form the foundation for your couple's bucket list. Find common ground, whether it's exploring new destinations, learning new skills, or achieving personal milestones.

Prioritise and Organise

Prioritise the goals based on mutual interest and urgency. Organise them into categories or themes, creating a structured outline for your list. This helps in setting a clear direction for your shared adventures.

Set Clear Goals

Phrase your goals in a clear and actionable manner. Use specific and measurable language to articulate what you want to achieve. This clarity will guide your efforts and make your accomplishments more tangible.

Create a Visual Representation

Transform your bucket list into a visual representation, whether it's a physical list, a digital document, or a vision board. Add images, quotes, or symbols that resonate with each goal, infusing a personalised touch.

Establish a Timeframe

Set realistic timeframes for achieving each goal. Whether they are short-term adventures or long-term dreams, having a timeline adds structure to your aspirations and helps in planning.

Regularly Revisit and Revise

Schedule periodic check-ins to revisit and revise your couples' bucket list. Celebrate the achievements, reflect on the experiences, and add new goals as your relationship evolves.

Embrace spontaneity:

While having a plan is essential, leave room for spontaneity. Some of the most memorable moments happen when you embrace unexpected opportunities and surprises together.

Creating a couple's bucket list is a collaborative and enriching endeavour that strengthens the connection between partners. It fuels shared excitement, fosters communication and provides a roadmap for a relationship filled with adventure and growth.

Quick Tips

Consistent Check-Ins: schedule regular check-ins to discuss feelings, desires, and any concerns. Consistency builds a strong foundation.

Embrace Playfulness: incorporate laughter and play into your relationship. Playful interactions strengthen the emotional connection.

Open Communication about Intimacy: discuss sexual desires openly and honestly. Creating a safe space for these conversations deepens intimacy.

Try New Things Together: From cooking classes to dance lessons, engaging in new activities together fosters shared experiences.

Remember, the key to a thriving relationship is continuous effort, communication and a willingness to grow together. Use this handbook as a starting point, adapting and expanding on the ideas to fit your unique connection. Here's to a journey of more profound love, understanding and pleasure for both of you. Cheers to a fulfilling and enduring relationship!